AF487933

EVERYONE HAS A SAM:

MEETING THE INNER CRITIC
AND RE·WRITING THE RULES

WRITTEN & ILLUSTRATED BY ROSI GREENBERG

Third Edition, 2024
ISBN: 979-8-218-17143-8
Library of Congress Control Number: 2023920712

for everyone who has an inner critic,
we see you.

keep going.

GOOD MORNING.

THIS IS ME AND THIS IS SAM.

SAM SAYS THIS IS A BAD DRAWING OF ME.

SAM IS MY INNER CRITIC.

SAM AND I ARE GOING TO
WRITE A BOOK TOGETHER.

SAM AND I
DO EVERYTHING
TOGETHER.
zoom

BUT SAM CAN BE REALLY MEAN SOMETIMES.

IN SOME WAYS, SAM IS MY OLDEST COMPANION.

OTHER PEOPLE COME AND GO
BUT SAM IS ALWAYS THERE.

I WISH HE WASN'T.

SAM WENT
TO INNER CRITIC
SCHOOL.

(SAM SAYS THE DESKS WERE ALL SYMMETRICAL
AND ALL THE SAME HEIGHT AND I'M BAD AT
DRAWING DESKS ANYWAYS)

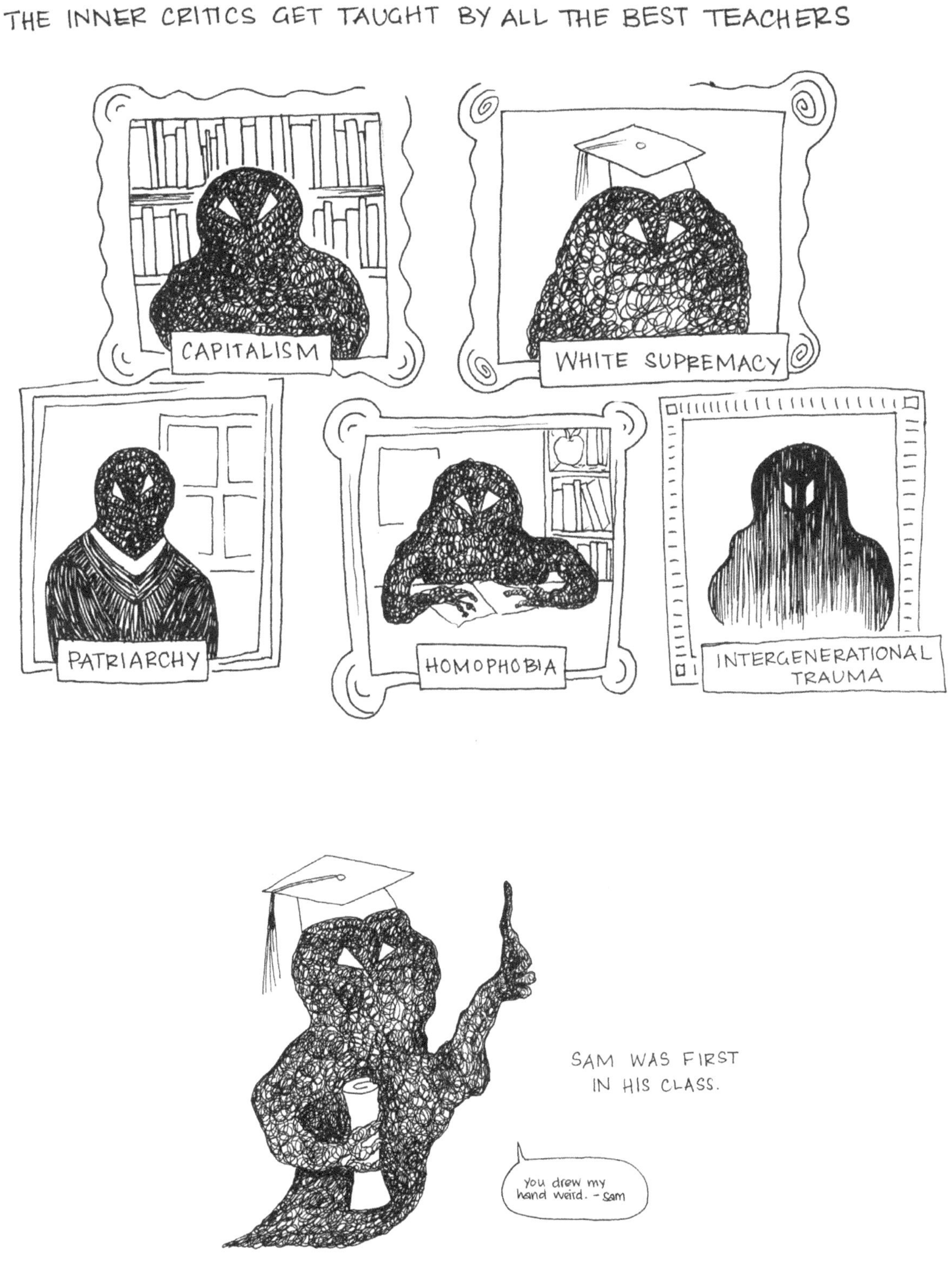

THE INNER CRITICS GET TAUGHT BY ALL THE BEST TEACHERS

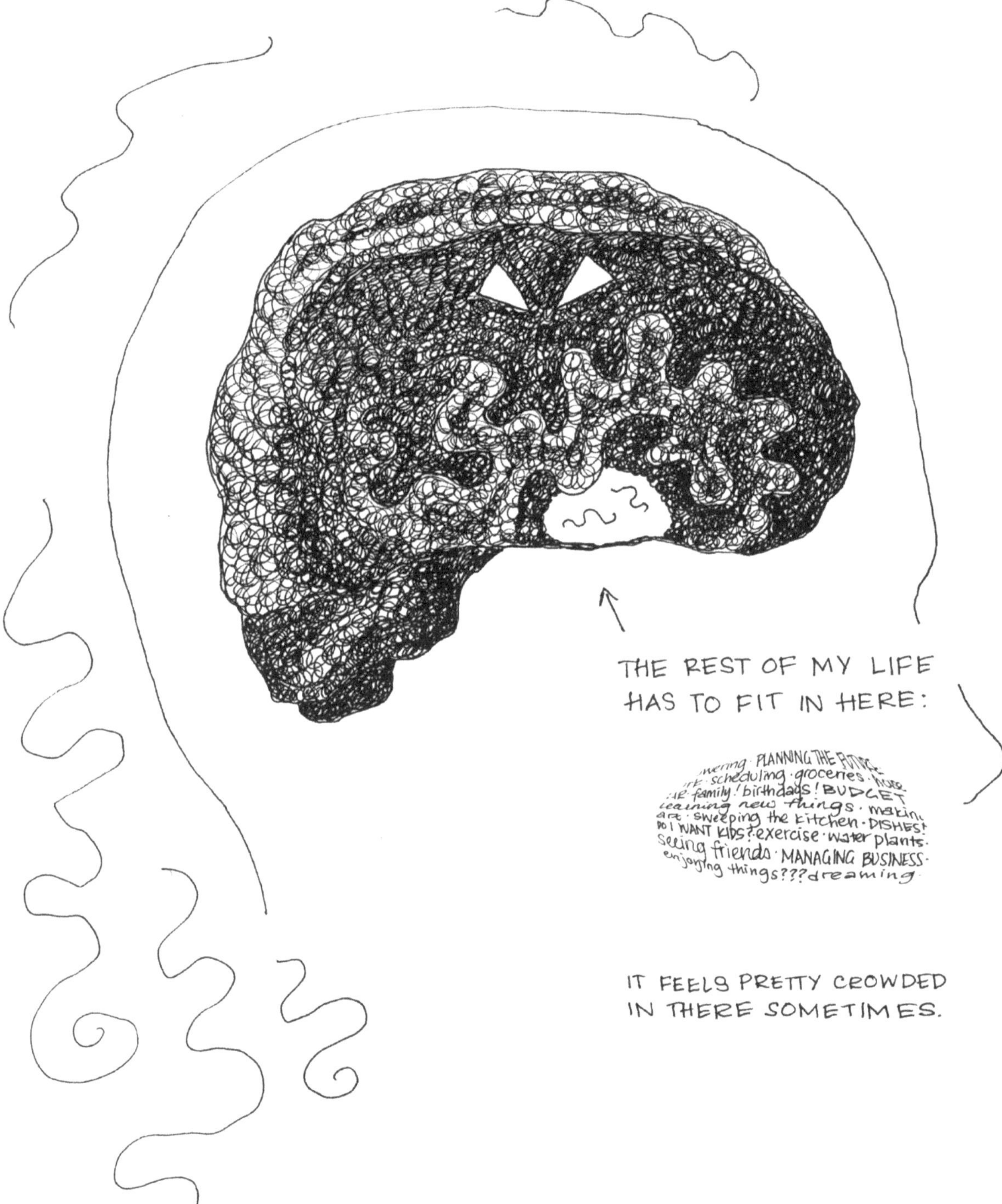

AT ANY GIVEN TIME, SAM TAKES UP APPROXIMATELY 95%
OF MY BRAIN SPACE.
THE REST OF MY LIFE
HAS TO FIT IN HERE:
...wering · PLANNING THE FUTURE·
...rk· scheduling · groceries· ...oto·
...r· family! birthdays! BUDGET
learning new things· makin...
art· sweeping the kitchen· DISHES!
DO I WANT KIDS? exercise· water plants·
seeing friends· MANAGING BUSINESS·
enjoying things??? dreaming·
IT FEELS PRETTY CROWDED
IN THERE SOMETIMES.

BUT AT LEAST
SAM HAS SPACE
TO RELAX.

JUST KIDDING.
SAM NEVER RELAXES.

I'VE TRIED VARIOUS THINGS TO GET RID OF SAM.

LIKE OVER·ACHIEVING

MEDITATING

EATING
ICE CREAM

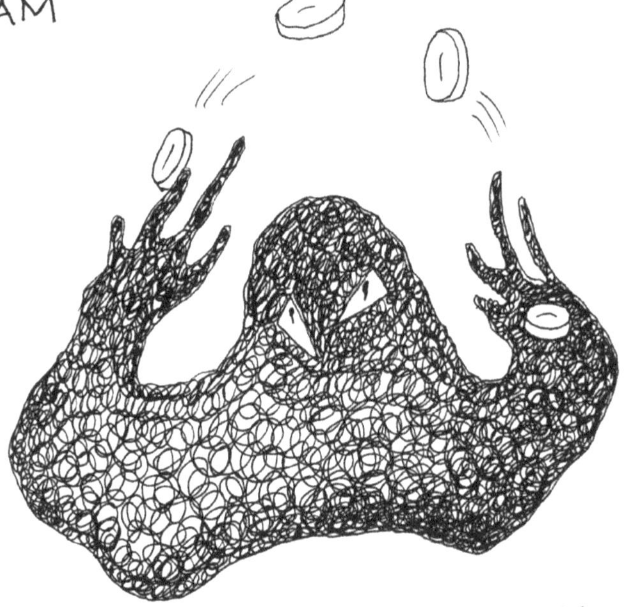

TAKING
ANTIDEPRESSANTS

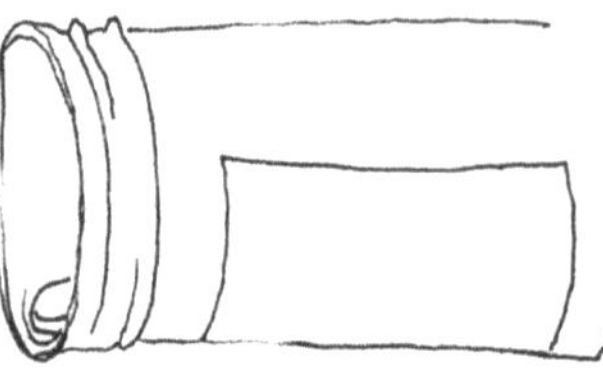

BUILDING WALLS
PLEADING
CRYING
SHOUTING
BEGGING
PRAYING

BUT SAM WILL NOT GO AWAY.

SAM HAS BEEN WITH ME
ALMOST MY WHOLE LIFE ...
PROM
PROM
PROM

I MET SAM IN KINDERGARTEN
AFTER I SPOKE AT SHOW·AND·TELL ONE DAY.
I went to Bill Clinton's auguration with my uncles!
Rosi, It's the In auguration, not the auguration! now sit down.
Anyways, we don't like children who miss 2 days of school.
You're wrong!
You're wrong!
You're wrong!
wrong!
You're wrong!
You're wrong!
You're wrong!
MY TEACHER YELLED A LOT.
KINDERGARTEN WAS VERY SCARY.

I WOULD HIDE IN THE BATHROOM
BECAUSE IT FELT SAFE IN THERE.

THAT'S WHERE SAM FOUND ME.

THAT WAS THE DAY SAM GRADUATED FROM CRITIC SCHOOL
AND WAS SENT TO FIND HIS HUMAN. HE WAS SO CRITICAL
HE LOOKED AT 4,324,905 PEOPLE BEFORE CHOOSING ME.

SAM CAME
FROM A STRONG
LINE OF CRITICS.

THOSE CRITICS WORKED FOR PEOPLE YOU'VE NEVER EVEN HEARD OF,
THAT'S HOW GOOD THEY WERE.

SAM APPRENTICED WITH MY MOM AND GRANDMA'S CRITICS. LUCKY US— THEIR JUDGMENTS WERE CAREFULLY HONED BY THEIR PARENTS' AND THEIR PARENTS PARENTS' CRITICS.

AND SO SAM LEARNED THE INSTRUCTIONS FOR LIFE.

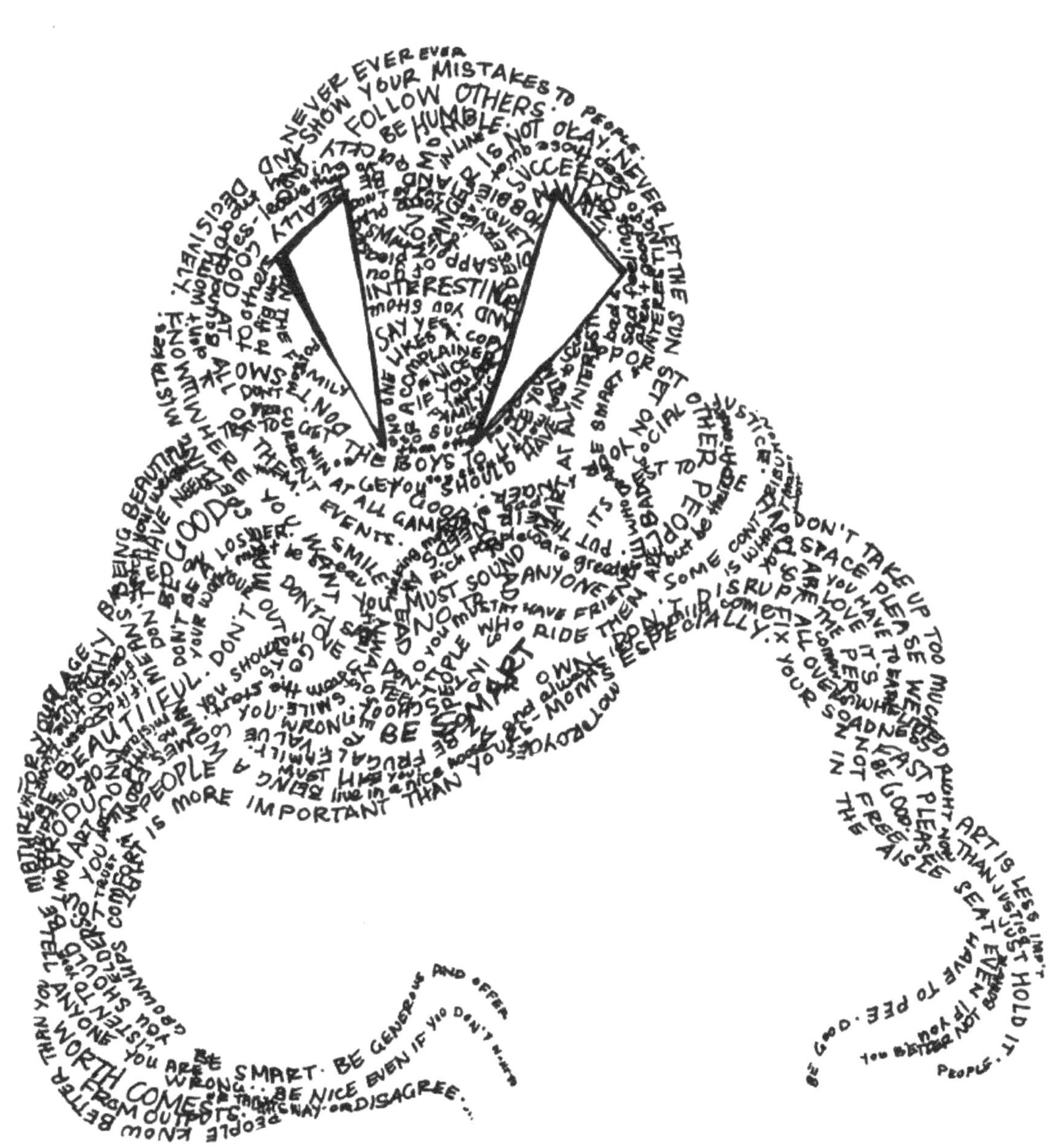

LAST YEAR SAM WAS SO LOUD
AND DOING HIS JOB SO WELL
THAT HE WAS ALL I COULD SEE.

AND HE STARTED GETTING
BIGGER

AND BIGGER

AND BIGGER.

AND I STARTED GETTING
SMALLER

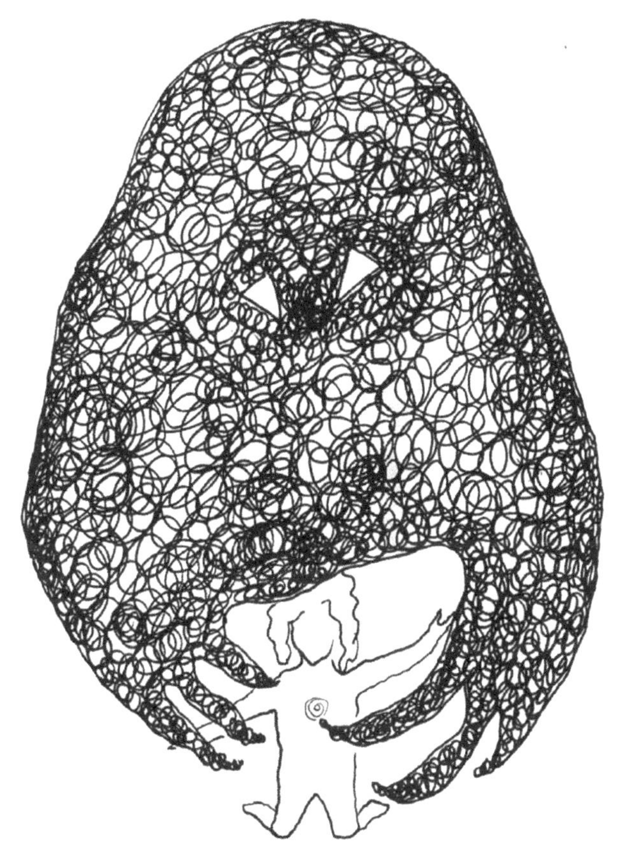

AND SMALLER

AND SMALLER.

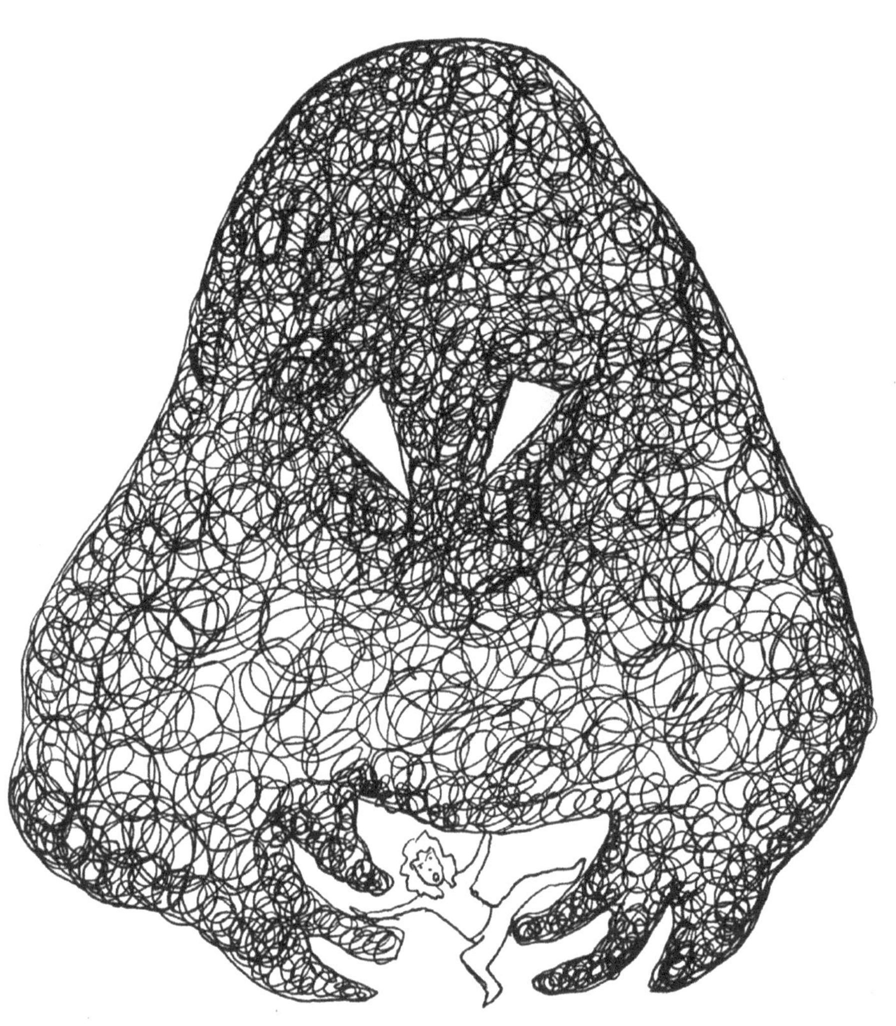

UNTIL THERE WAS ALMOST NO ME LEFT.

I COULD BARELY BREATHE.

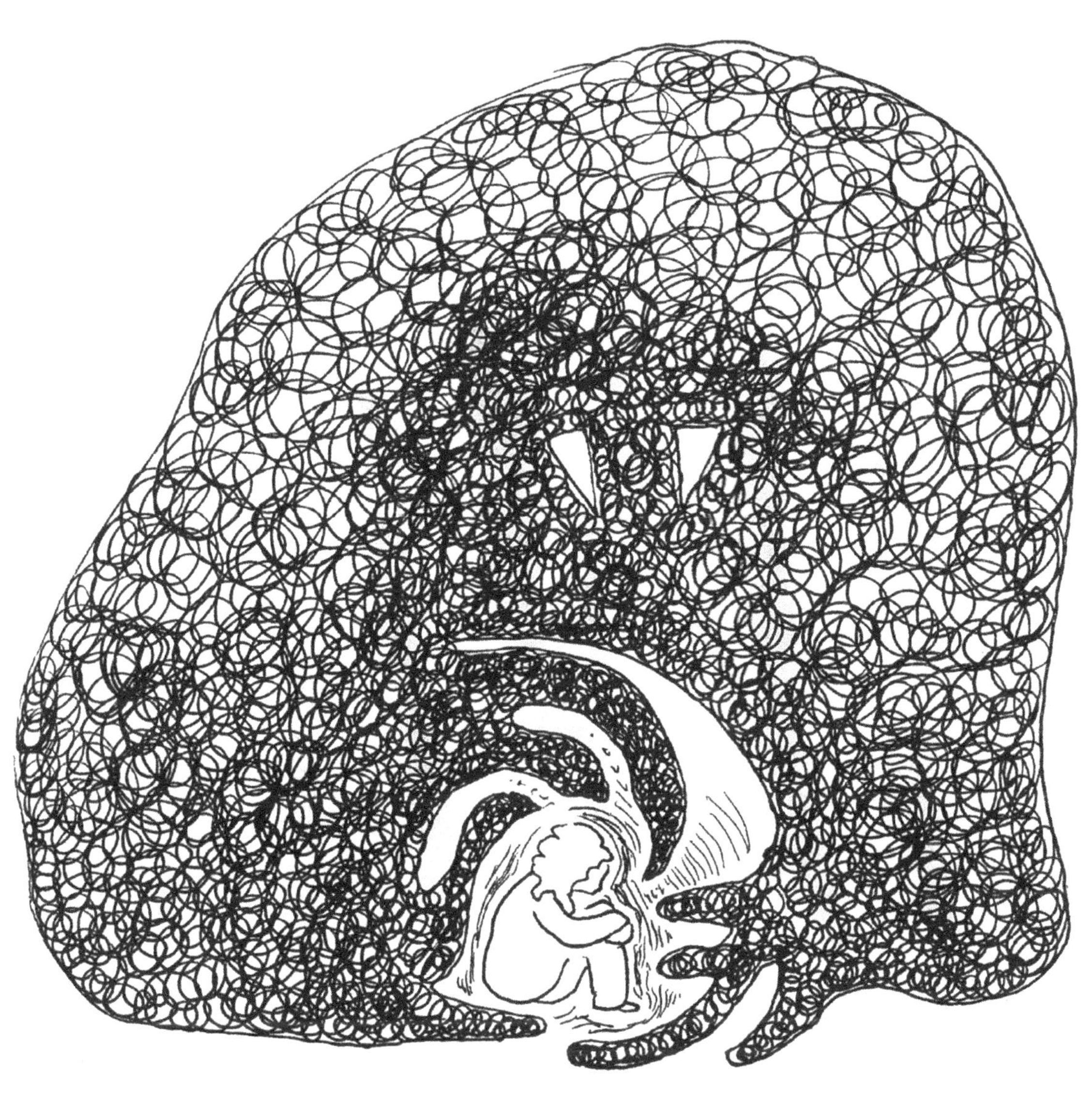

IT WAS VERY DARK IN THERE.

IN THAT PLACE, I COULDN'T
FEEL ANYTHING.

IN THAT PLACE, EVEN ICE CREAM DIDN'T TASTE GOOD.

FOR MONTHS
IT FELT LIKE
IT WAS JUST ME
AND MY JOURNAL
AND MY PENS.

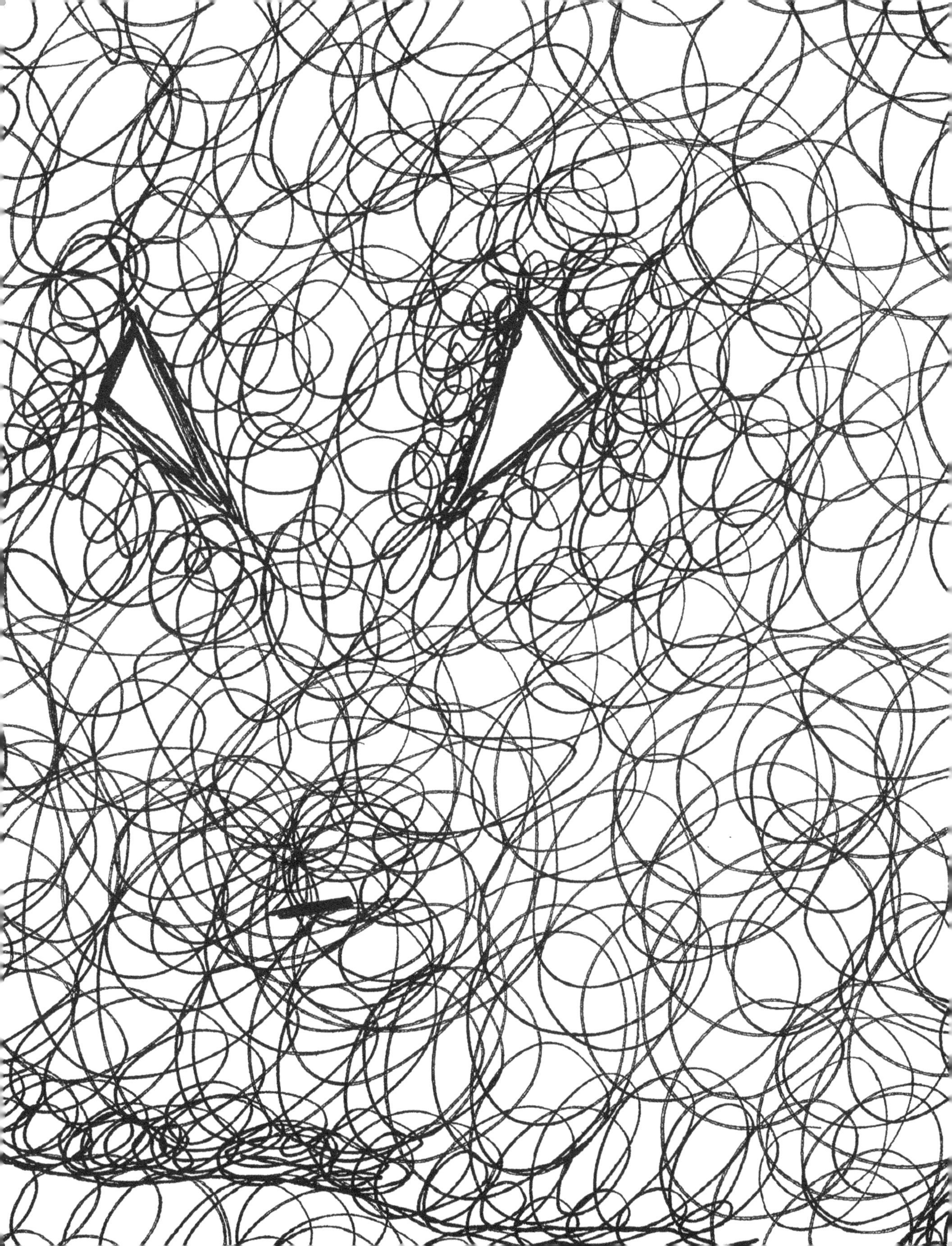

THEN
  ONE DAY,
      IN THE MIDST OF MY DARKNESS,
          A FRIEND SUGGESTED I DRAW SAM.

AND IT TURNED OUT THAT MY JOURNAL AND PENS
WERE EXACTLY ALL I NEEDED

DRAWING HIM HAD NEVER OCCURRED TO ME

BUT ONCE HE WAS ON PAPER, HE WASN'T SO SCARY.

HE WAS BASICALLY JUST A SQUIGGLE.

(I HAPPEN TO LOVE SQUIGGLES)

Dear Sam,

I want you to be able to relax on that beach and not bother me so much. What would you need in order to retire?

- Rosi

I CAN'T RELAX ON THE BEACH BECAUSE

IF I DO, EVERYTHING COULD FALL APART

FALL APART.

FALL
A
P
A
R
T

PEOPLE MIGHT HATE YOU
YOU'LL HAVE NO MONEY
YOU WON'T GET TO HAVE A FAMILY
FALLING APART WOULD BE TERRIBLE.
YOU'LL BE ALONE FOREVER
YOU'LL BE STUCK FOREVER

AND THEN I REALIZED:

SAM WAS ACTUALLY
JUST REALLY SCARED.

your hair is too long.
your hair is too short.
you clog the drain dummy
you should have showered yesterday.
your skin is getting dry.
you smell.
hurry up you're wasting water.
figure out what to do with your life. now.
you're not being creative enough. use this time well.
you don't have good soap or shampoo. why don't you buy yourself nice things?
you don't deserve to spend money on yourself
you don't clean the bathroom enough.
you're lazy.
you're getting fat.
you're a moocher you should get your own CSA
stop taking so much from friends.
you're so lazy for not toasting it longer.
you don't deserve a break get back to work.
this tastes bad.
you should have toasted it longer!
you're eating too many calories!
you should have made soup.
you shouldn't take so long for lunch.
you're selfish.
use this time more productively.
You should stop eating bread!
what will you do about the boo you should've decided already.
you should make your own mayonnaise.
you didn't get back to Marshall in a timely manner.
why don't you have nice plates you love.
you should have gone left back there.
you're going so slow.
you're late
you're always late for friends.
So and so is a better biker than you.
(you're so indecisive)
Raffi is a better biker than you. (be specific for the book stupid)
you're slouching. you always slouch.
you're selfish - you should have let that pedestrian cross first.
this bike drawing is terrible and you look like you're wearing a leotard. you never wear leotards. no one should publish this.
TURNED OUT, HE THOUGHT HE'D BEEN PROTECTING ME THE WHOLE TIME.
you need a haircut.
they're all real grown ups and you're just pretending.
you have a snaggletooth.
you're so unprofessional
that was a dumb thing to say.
why should they ever work with you again?
literally anyone could do this job better.
why bother.
you have nothing to offer here.
you're only in this for the money.
you don't care about anything real.
you're unimpressive.
you look tired.
you got all this wrong. this isn't what I say. you're doing this for show & ego. you're nothing.

you are precious to me. you're my only human.
if I keep you perfect everyone will like you and no one will hurt you again
WOW...
I GUESS...
THANK YOU, SAM.

but Sam, i basically _did_ fall apart this year.
and i felt small & lonely & disconnected & IMPERFECT
and guess what?

i survived.

IN FACT,

IT TAKES A VERY STRONG PERSON TO
BE OKAY FALLING APART.

in fact...
FALLING APART IS
A PART OF LIFE.

SOMETIMES
YOU HAVE TO
FALL
APART

TO GET BACK UP AGAIN.

SO NOW I LISTEN WHEN I DECIDE SAM'S
`GUIDANCE` IS HELPFUL

BUT AS FOR HIS INSTRUCTIONS FOR LIFE...

I MAKE MY OWN.
there is no pressure.
it's OK to have a VOICE & BE POWERFUL!
YOU ARE GOOD NO MATTER WHAT
i am important and unimportant at the same time
you are allowed to be unproductive
it's okay to CRY
it's okay to be SAD or ANGRY
i love ME!
I LOVE YOU
it's okay to take UP SPACE
it's okay to do nothing some days
sometimes really ann and th okay
I AM WORTHY
you get to make MISTAKES
i give myself permission to fart in public without embarrassment. sorry y'all - it's just my body.
YOU DON'T HAVE TO PLEASE PEOPLE TO BE LOVED
it's OK to doubt
i get have wants and needs (& ask them if they a always
you don't have to be any different than you are - i lo

okay to say dumb things sometimes!

I can make messes !!

& I LOVE THEM!

sometimes my hair looks like a total mess too and that is okay.

...y to be LOUD

I'M ALLOWED to look ugly.

my body is good just the way it is.

IT'S OK TO FEEL STUCK SOMETIMES

IT'S OK TO FEEL LONELY — (you're never really alone)

it's okay to feel tired.

you don't have to do everything all at once

I'm ...ing!

I'm measured by no means — certainly not by what I produce.

NO MATTER WHAT.

IT'S OKAY TO NOT KNOW THE ANSWER

a good daughter is whatever you ARE - you don't need to be anything different.

my opinion matters and it's okay to share it — even when others disagree.

you, me.

AND SO CAN YOU.

the

end

OR MAYBE JUST THE BEGINNING!

Acknowledgements

thank you Mom & Polly for teaching me independence, power, and knowing I'm special, in addition to teaching Sam. Your role modeling for me how to be one's own woman (person) in the world is powerful, and I am forever grateful.

thank you Dove for showing me how to believe in oneself as an artist

thank you Raffi, Zoe, Joey, Mozi and Yotam for siblingship on the journey. And to Fahad, Axelle, Houman, Albane, Megan, Anita, Aditi, Erich, Elle, Sarah, Karen, Nick, Marya, Aliya, Claris, Lindsay, Anjali, Georgie, Rebecca and Barbary, Duvy & Dan for friendship & love. Thank you for holding me in some of the hardest moments, celebrating with me in the joys, and being a phone call away for everything in between. I love you guys.

thank you Marshall for seeing me & suggesting I draw Sam. The friendship, coaching, sushi and discussions of the Eumenides were life-saving.

thank you to Mimi Sternlicht and Christina Peabody of Foundation House Residency for believing in me as an artist early on – you helped me believe in myself.

thank you Alex Souksby and Mom Tri of Artist Residency Thailand – Alex, thank you for letting me build a 15-ft tall inner critic in your office and experiment with the fourth graders' inner meanies. And for the encouragement.

Thank you to:

KONU – Michael Koehler
   & Tim O'Brien
Mobius – Amy & Erica Fox
Dragonfly – Reb & B

Sherine Hamdy
   Joseph & crew

Cliff Barry & Vicki Woodard
   – Shadow Work

Farayi Chipungu & Ron Heifetz – Adaptive Leadership

Dick Schwartz – Internal Family Systems

Marshall Ganz – Public
   & Sarah ElRaheb Narrative

to   Ryan Hampton, Mobilize Recovery
        & my coaching crew : deep gratitude.

Thank you family tribe, especially Miggie.

Thank you Grandpa & Wanda for ever-loving support.

Thank you Zalman for giving me life and showing me
    there is more to it than I initially thought.

Thank you to everyone who gave me publishing advice
    and editorial support (zoe! kath! Jason!)
and to all the artists and writers who have inspired me.

Thank you to Debby Pollak for being my first
    beloved art teacher & for helping art become a home.

& Sam says I probably forgot someone and if that's you—
I'm sorry!

and to Sam: thank you for being my oldest companion.
I couldn't have gotten here without you.

Love, Rosi

SOMETIMES THE MAGIC YOU BRING
TO YOUR STRUGGLES
IS EXACTLY WHAT THE WORLD NEEDS.

love Rosi

About the Author

Rosi Greenberg is an Artist of Leadership Development. As founder and CEO of Drawn to Lead, she empowers leaders at all levels to articulate their stories, rediscover their inner strength, and cultivate more compassionate and creative organizations. With a Master's in Public Policy from the Harvard Kennedy School and expertise in Internal Family Systems, Shadow Work, and mediation, Rosi specializes in the emotional dimensions of leadership. Her other artistic creations include ceramics, drawing/painting/collage, and magical live-scribing documentation of conversations. Her work bridges artistry and leadership, and nurtures profound empathy for self and other. The oldest daughter of a single mother, Rosi grew up in Philadelphia, PA and currently lives in the sunny foothills of Boulder, Colorado.

visit **www.everyonehasasam.com**
to contribute your critic drawing to our growing gallery, and find resources & events.

email **rosi.greenberg@drawntolead.org**
for permissions, workshops or speaking engagements, and/or just to connect.